How Work Works

Matthew Elliott

A catalogue record for this book is available from the National Library of Australia

Independent Consultation and representation
Workshop/incursions
contact us now at www.howworkworks.com

Copyright © 2022 Matthew Elliott
All rights reserved.
Second Edition
ISBN-13: 978-1-922727-54-1

Linellen Press
265 Boomerang Road
Oldbury, Western Australia
www.linellenpress.com.au

Contents

Contents iii
Introduction 1
   Disclaimer.. 4
So who am I? 5
Chapter One - Awards 7
Chapter Two - Workplace Agreements 17
Chapter Three - BOOTs Test 24
Chapter Four - Hourly/composite rate/annual salary ... 26
Chapter Five - Workplace Health and Safety 30
Chapter Six - Workers Compensation 38
Chapter Seven - Probation 45
Chapter Eight - Letters of Offer 48
Chapter Nine - Employment Contracts 50
Chapter Ten - Workplace policies 53
Chapter Eleven - Leave 55
Chapter Twelve - Casual Conversion. 61
Chapter Thirteen - Meetings 63
Chapter Fourteen - Employment Termination ... 67
Chapter Fifteen - Superannuation 75
Chapter Sixteen - Pay Rises and CPI 79
Chapter Seventeen - The NES 81
Chapter Eighteen - The 38 Hour Working Week ... 83
Chapter Nineteen - Unions 86
Chapter Twenty - Bullying 89
Chapter Twenty-one - Payslips 92
Chapter Twenty-two - The Gig Economy 97

Introduction

I've written this book hoping to give some insight to the reader on "How Work Works" and how I understand workplaces work. In it, I try to explain a worker's rights and an employer's rights and their responsibilities in Australian workplaces.

Industrial laws and the legislation that controls our workplaces are detailed, complex and living. By living, I mean they evolve and change regularly as court cases set precedents, as governments change, and as legislation is altered or introduced. They live.

This makes it entirely possible that some of the personal experiences I share here are now currently incorrect or incomplete in their explanation. I am happy to be corrected, and I mean no harm to any reader if a mistake has occurred.

At the very least, I hope this book starts a conversation on the education of workplace rights and obligations. Then more experienced and professional people can start to educate workers, new and old, managers and owners on workplace rights and responsibilities.

I no longer believe this education of workplace rights should be completed by organisations with vested interests in workplaces. For these organisations, profit and profitability come first. There needs to be an independent organisation or person(s) explaining these rights.

Our working lives will, and does, govern everything we do as adults – where we live; where we holiday; if we can afford a family, or even afford to retire. I believe working must be in the top three life choices we have to make, yet it appears our education on How Work Works is very, very limited.

My first two children, who hit the workforce at sixteen while still studying, knew nothing about "How Work Works".

One daughter was educated at an expensive private school, the other in one of the top five state schools. Both are in Perth. Both scored over 90 ATAR's, so they were good students and smart people. But they had no idea of working rights and responsibilities.

They know they must work. They have been educated to work effectively, but they both had no understanding on how work works.

Both had terrible experiences in their first jobs. Each time, I had to intervene to ensure fairness was reached. Our first jobs are our most important jobs in my opinion. The way we are treated in the first few employment experiences can influence our working lives.

In conjunction with this publication, I will be working on two other aspects of service: an independent consultancy and a school incursion presentation educating new workers. This presentation will also be available for backpackers, refugees and new arrivals to Australia. (I will also be conducting presentations at regular intervals around Perth at different locations.)

Disclaimer

This book is not written as a detailed and accurate account of all rights and responsibilities in the Australian workplace. Each chapter could indeed be a book in its own right.

This book simply is a layman sharing his experiences and personal knowledge. I am no expert on industrial rights and responsibilities, just a worker.

So who am I?

I am a 54-year-old worker; a single dad with three kids. I have a trade certificate.

I have worked and been employed in various roles within the health care, transport, manufacturing, agriculture, hospitality, tourism, and warehousing industries. In the past, I have been a self-employed person employing my own staff.

Currently, I am working on a mine site in remote Western Australia, so I am *just* a worker, like most of my audience I trust.

I have been, and currently am, a safety rep. I have also been the elected shop steward (union delegate) and have worked within the trade union movement.

I have worked day shifts, night shifts, afternoon shifts over a 7-day roster; worked weekends and all public holidays; in isolated and in city-based locations. I have worked as a solo employee as well as being a member of large teams.

My 'uniforms' have been a suit and tie to hi-vis and steel caps. I have been employed as a casual, full-time and part-timer. Also as a contractor.

I have been promoted; been employee of the month, and of the year. I have been terminated and self-terminated. I have managed staff, employed staff, and terminated staff.

I have been overpaid, underpaid and not paid. I have never been on workers' compensation for an extended period. My workers' compensation experience is a few days off work for running repairs, e.g. stitches.

I honestly believe my diverse employment experiences have exposed me to many different workplace management styles and industrial laws, which has helped me write about my experiences in the hope of helping others.

Chapter One

Awards

What are Awards?

I have asked many people this question about our workplaces, and most have no idea what an Award is. This really surprises me as Awards are the basis, or the foundations, of all our employment terms and conditions.

Every Australian worker has their employment terms and conditions, or at the very least, their minimum employment terms and conditions outlined and governed by an industry-based Award.

It's very important to note that Awards are industry-based, meaning that all employees of a particular industry will generally have an Award. For example, chefs work in the area known as the 'hospitality industry'. Their minimum employment terms and conditions can be found in the Federal Hospitality Industry (General) Award. 2010

In my home state's industrial system – Western Australia – that same chef may find their employment terms and conditions are governed by the state-based Award called the *'Restaurant Tea Rooms and Catering Workers Award'*. Alternatively, it may fall under the

'Hotel and Tavern Award'.

It can be confusing to figure out which Award establishes a worker's employment terms and conditions. To help, there are usually clauses that explain which industries an Award covers. This is called 'coverage'.

Every Award has a coverage clause. It is usually one of the first clauses of the Award or, at the very least, in the top five clauses.

The coverage clause attempts to explain which workers are captured or covered by that Award.

Using the example of a chef again, a chef may find their employment conditions could be established by a few Awards in the federal system; for example, a chef may have their employment terms and conditions covered by the Hospitality Industry (general) Award, The Restaurant Industry Award, Vehicle Repairs, Services and Retail Award maybe even the Maritime Offshore Oil and Gas Award.

It's important to note that when we are attempting to establish which Award we are covered by, we need to remember that awards are *'industry-based'*, not *'occupational-based'*.

The main criteria for establishing which industry we are working within is the employer's main business activity.

If this chef was working at a roadhouse where the primary business activity is selling car products and fuel, then the chef could be covered by the *Vehicle Repairs, Services and Retail Award* due to the business's primary operation.

However, if the same chef worked in a pub next door to the roadhouse, the chef would find themselves covered by the Hospitality Industry (General) Award, as the primary business activity is food and beverage.

I have discussed federal and state-based industrial system awards regarding our chef. So, if all employees are covered by industry-based awards, how do we know if we are working within the federal or state-based industrial system, and why do we need to know this?

> **REMEMBER:**
> *Awards are industry-based,*
> *not occupation-based.*

State and Federal Awards vary. Additionally, if a worker or an employer decides to lodge an application in the industrial court system seeking a settlement to a dispute, be aware the court systems also vary.

To discover if we are in the federal or state system is simple – but occasionally, the following solution does not work.

If your employer is state-based, you could fall into the state system. An example would be a teacher, a health care provider in a state-run hospital, or you could work in the state's public service.

Remember the example of the chef moving from

job to job, hence changing the Award they could be covered under. The same could be for a nurse who worked in a state-run hospital then started work for a private provider that has branches or clinics in various states. The nurse could change industrial systems from state to federal.

If your employer is a national employer, or the employer has set up their business to run as a PTY LTD – proprietary limited entity – then you could fall into the federal system. 'Proprietary Limited' is a way to set up a business for taxation purposes, as I understand it.

An example of how this solution does not always work in Western Australia, my home state: local government bodies, which are state-based, do not operate as PTY LTDs, but they fall into the federal system because the government of the day a few decades ago forfeited their right to be industrially responsible for local government to the federal system.

This has had a major impact on the workers as, in my opinion, the state award and industrial system is far superior compared to the federal award and system.

Any questions about this call me, and we can find out together.

What do Awards establish in our employment?

Awards set the minimum employment terms and conditions and do this by a range of clauses within

them. For example, Awards can
- outline rostering patterns,
- leave entitlements,
- wages and classifications,
- apprenticeship and training pay rates,
- the process to be followed concerning consultation about changes in the workplace
- flexibility,
- redundancy,
- span of hours,
- ordinary hours,
- penalty rates, and
- allowances, to name a few.

But what *are* all those things mentioned above? What do they mean? What are ordinary hours and span of hours? Flexibility? Wages and classification?

Let's look at a few. It would be possible to write an entire book solely about Awards and each clause and its meanings. But that is inconsistent with my intentions of this book, so I will pick a few of the important clauses and try and unpack them a little more. Any more questions, call me.

I am going to use the chef example again.

Classification

The minimum level a chef (trade qualified) can be paid under the Federal *Hospitality General Industry Award* is: Classification Level 4, Grade 3. As this chef's responsibilities grow, skills and experience develop, a chef can be paid at Level 5, Grade 4 or the highest; Level 6, Grade 5.

You would expect that a head chef who is responsible for ordering, staff rostering and is highly skilled would (or should) be paid at the top rate as set by the Federal Hospitality General Award at Level 6, Grade 5.

These steps within the pay scale are called the classification structure. We are classified as workers within this structure, depending on our training, skill levels and the tasks we are asked to complete.

This is also how we move between classification levels to receive higher pay. As responsibilities grow, wages grow. Well, wages *should* grow.

Some Awards I have read are absolutely specific about the duties to be completed or expected to be completed for a particular classification, and therefore the coinciding pay level. Other Awards are not so specific about the duties expected to fit into a classification. So each Award varies.

Next to the classification structure is usually the minimum pay level that a worker should receive for a particular classification. So, our chef deemed to be level 4 grade 3 receives (currently at the time of writing, but this changes) $862.50 per week or $22.70 per hour for 'ordinary hours' worked.

What are ordinary hours, I hear you say? ... Well, read on.

Span of hours or Ordinary Hours

In most Awards I have read, they explain what the *'span of hours'* is. Sometimes, other terms are used like 'ordinary hours', but they usually have the same meaning.

The span of hours is the time when an employer can roster a worker to come to work. For example, span of hours could be described as between 6am to 6pm Monday to Friday.

That's not to say a worker can be rostered for 12-hour days, 5 days a week. It means that the standard 38 hours work required of a full-time worker can be rostered anywhere within these *'span of hours'* of 6am to 6pm, Monday to Friday.

Many of us, however, will or do work outside this example of 6am to 6pm, Monday to Friday. What happens when our chef works until 11pm at night?

When a worker completes work, or is rostered, outside the Award's described ordinary hours or span of hours, then penalty rates or weekend rates are applied, as described by a particular Award.

For example, if a worker is rostered to work Thursday afternoon from 3pm to 9.30pm and the span of hours is described in their Award as 6am to 6pm Monday to Friday, then that worker has worked outside the span of the ordinary hours for 3.5 hours. So those 3.5 hours worked should attract a penalty rate as described by that Award.

Hours worked outside the 'span of hours' or 'ordinary hours' as described can attract penalty rates or extra wages depending on what the Award states.

It's never a yes/no answer.

The span of hours or ordinary hours as described in any Award can and do vary from industry to industry, and so these hours can and do change from Award to Award.

I recall reading an Award describing the span of hours as between 5am to 11pm Monday to Sunday.

Definitions

Most Awards I have read, and other employment documents, have what is called a 'Definitions' clause. These are, again, usually located at the beginning of the Award, or can be in the top five clauses.

Definitions are there to clarify and to prevent a dispute about the meaning of what a certain term or words mean in that particular Award or document.

Using the *Hospitality Industry (General) Award* again, the definitions explain, for example, what a restaurant or resort is. Funnily enough, the definitions list also includes *spread of hours*.

What is *spread of hours?!* I hear you cry.

It's just another term for *span of hours* or *ordinary hours*.

Another example of definition is 'immediate family'. So, whenever the term appears or is referred to in an Award or a document, the definition explains what or who is considered an immediate family member. This term 'immediate family' is usually used in a clause referring to carers leave and compassionate leave.

The definitions included in Awards are very

important as they relate to the employment conditions within a specific work industry. If you're ever unsure of what a term means, it's important to check what the definition clause of the Award or document states.

In future chapters, and as I go along, I will explain some other clauses that can be found in Awards. But as I already said, I think a whole book could be written on just Awards, so I do not wish to get too bogged down on this.

A couple of other things about Awards before we complete this chapter.

When you start work with a new employer, you should be told, usually in writing, which Award the employer uses to establish your employment terms and conditions.

This seems obvious, but in my experience, it rarely occurs, particularly when I have worked for your 'mum and dad' style operations. Larger organisations with HR teams usually do this, but not always.

Your Award must be made available to you in the workplace. These days, this is usually done electronically, but a hard copy is the best way.

I think a hard copy is best because you can take that copy to someone to discuss a particular clause and what it means. It's easier. It can also promote debate which is a great thing.

When reading an Award, I strongly encourage you to read the whole clause and not just a sub-section that works for you. The whole clause may have a sub-clause that excludes another sub-clauses or refers to another clause in the Award, or even other documents that exclude the sub-clause that works for you. Yes, it can be a rabbit warren but remember, read the whole clause.

Awards change from time to time. The most recent change I can remember was the introduction of an unpaid domestic violence leave clause to all Awards. So, stay in touch and update your copy annually. In 2010, the whole Award system was reduced from around 1,500 Awards to a couple of hundred plus.

Awards can be daunting to read, interpret and understand. If you are ever unsure, seek a second opinion or just call me.

So, in this chapter and as a conclusion, know that Awards are industry-based and they establish the minimum terms and conditions of employment for workers.

Basically, an employer just can't make up employment terms and conditions, and neither can the worker.

What happens when an employer increases the terms and conditions of employment in workplace?

Well, that's the next chapter ...

Chapter Two

Workplace Agreements

In Chapter One, we discussed industry-based Awards and how these 'industrial instruments' set workers minimum standards and conditions of employment.

('Industrial instrument' is the accepted term or name for any document that can have influence over employment conditions.)

But Awards are not the only industrial instrument that can have influence over a worker's employment terms and conditions. Workplace Agreements are an example of another industrial instrument.

Workplace agreements can be referred to by many different names.

You may come across employers who might call these any one of the following:

- Negotiated Workplace Agreement,
- Enterprise Workplace Agreement,
- Certified Agreement,
- Enterprise Bargaining Agreement

… and the list goes on, but they are all the same thing and have the same outcome.

These agreements are established when workers, and possibly their representative (usually a union), sit down with an employer to negotiate and agree on the terms and conditions of employment for a specific workplace or employer.

As Awards are industry-specific documents, these agreements are therefore usually employer-specific.

Amendments are rarely made to Awards, and they generally remain active for an extended period.

Agreements, however, have an expiry date and therefore are updated regularly.

This is an advantage, I believe, to both the employer and workers, as it provides more flexibility to be adaptable and respond to changes that occur in all business environments, such as changes in technology, or an increase or decrease in product demand or competition.

Just as employers' environments can change, so do workers' environments, such as a rise in the cost of living, or skills need updating, or we complete further training. We are all in a state of constant flux regarding change.

Agreements have clauses exactly like, or similar to, Awards. By law, all agreements must have certain clauses or minimum standards set outlining and explaining workers' rights, for example, consultation, flexibility in employment, redundancy etc.

Agreements, however, can expand on clauses to include other entitlements to workers that Awards have initially failed to cover.

For example, all Awards include a clause referring

to an entitlement to workers to access unpaid domestic violence leave. There are many workplaces, however, that have successfully negotiated agreements that have domestic violence leave as a *paid* entitlement. This has been achieved by negotiating a workplace agreement.

Awards set the minimum terms and conditions of employment. Agreements, however, are designed to raise standards above Award conditions.

Agreements are complicated and difficult industrial documents to negotiate and establish. There are numerous forms of legislation and court judgements that influence how this process is completed. For example, when the Fair Work Act legislation was passed and came into effect as law in 2009/2010, it mentioned that negotiations for any workplace agreement must occur with 'good faith bargaining'.

But what does or what did 'good faith bargaining' even mean? How does it apply to workplace negotiations?

For me, it means we must tell the truth; we should not threaten parties to advance a position by either ceasing work or withdrawing work and so on. We must act in good faith.

So how does it work?

As I mentioned earlier, industrial law establishing a workplace agreement is a very complex legal process. The intention of this book is to explain this in simple layman terms, and, as a layman myself, here is my take on how the process works on negotiating a workplace agreement.

1. A workforce gets together and decides they want to negotiate a new agreement with their employer. It can be the first time this workplace has had an agreement, or to replace an agreement that is or is about to or has already expired.
2. The workforce decides what they want – a wish list if you like. These lists can include:

    - pay rises every year
    - an increase in employer super contributions
    - six months paid maternity leave
    - paid domestic violence leave
    - increase in redundancy packages
    - paid training leave
    - restructure of progression steps through a classification, etc. etc.

    It can be anything really. As such, I describe it as a wish list.
3. There are non-permitted matters that cannot be placed in agreements or on wish lists, and they are anything that contradicts an existing legislation or is illegal. Which makes sense.
4. Once this wish list is decided upon, the

workers then inform management they wish to enter into negotiations for a workplace agreement.
5. All parties meet. Workers present their wish list, and the parties negotiate until they find common ground, and come to an agreement.
6. When this agreement is reached, it is registered with the appropriate legal body.
7. You now have a workplace agreement.

This is a very simplistic version of how these documents are created. It is, or can be, a very difficult and lengthy process. This all depends on how workers and employers conduct themselves, as well as the wish list provided.

Understand that a worker's wish list can be met with an employer's wish list. After all, this is a negotiation process, and both parties have the right to present a wish list they want to negotiate.

There are also several specific forms that must be used at certain stages of the process to allow each party time to consider the agreement without having to feel pressured or forced to decide straight away. If we fail to supply the right form, at the right time, for the right length of time, the whole process could fall over at time of registration.

You may need also need to prove good faith bargaining.

How do you do this?

This is usually done via correspondence: meeting minutes and witnesses. So it's important to keep detailed records of meetings and negotiations.

Ballots must occur in the workplace to get an agreement up ... so to speak. I think the balloting system is: only 51% of the workforce has to vote for a ballot to be recognised. And of that 51%, only 51% must vote yes for an agreement to get over the line. So it's important to vote.

Anyone can be invited to the negotiation table to represent either party. Understand that there are people and organisations who negotiate agreements for a living, day in, day out.

Either party can use a representative at the negotiation table. You may need to be prepared to negotiate with a professional.

In my opinion, not all employers treat workers with respect. Some employers present and push their own agreements at the table that may lower the conditions and entitlements that a worker is currently receiving.

In 2020, I started work for an organisation that presented a Workplace Agreement to me, and I was informed that agreement was being used to set my employment terms and conditions.

The agreement was registered in another business's trading name, which had expired eight years earlier, and did not have my job position in the classification structure. It had a very low pay rate.

In Chapter One, I discussed the term 'spread of hours or ordinary hours. I have seen employers attempt to change the spread of hours from, say, 6am to 6pm Monday to Friday to 5am to 11pm Monday to Sunday. This type of change could eliminate the requirement to pay any penalties to workers they may have been receiving in the past.

Simple changes in workplace agreements can affect workers' entitlements drastically, and usually go unnoticed. I have fallen foul of such a simple oversight, and it related to an agreement being drafted in one year. Negations dragged over to a new year, but the drafted agreement dates were not updated. This had a significant impact.

This is not a process to be taken lightly or easily. Negotiations can drag on for months, and that may be a tactic of a party at the table. If you get it wrong, it can have wide-reaching and long-term effects on current and new workers that you may never be able to regain.

I must say, however, these agreements, when treated with respect by all parties, can have a sincere, positive effect in a workplace and, in fact, a community.

One last thing: these agreements can be read in conjunction with an industry-based Award or can be what is termed as 'standalone' documents. Standalone documents mean that the industry-based Award is silent. It no longer influences your employment terms and conditions (minus the absolute minimum conditions of employment set by the Fair Work Act).

Chapter Three

BOOTs Test

In Chapter One, I repeatedly stated that Awards set or establish the minimum employment standards workers in Australia can be employed under. These Awards govern various rights and responsibilities in workplaces and detail information specific to a particular industry.

In Chapter Two, I outlined that workers and employers can elect to negotiate a workplace agreement to either work alongside, or in conjunction with, an Award, or to completely replace an Award. These Workplace Agreements usually can, and do, improve on the minimum employment standards set by an Award.

A tool that was introduced to ensure negotiated workplace agreements meet and/or exceed the minimum standards set by Awards is called a BOOTs test.

BOOTs is an acronym for 'Better off Overall Test'.

This test is applied by Fair Work Australia Commissioners and their associates when considering an application to register a negotiated workplace agreement.

The concept, as I understand it, is when workers in a workplace have voted to have their employment conditions governed by an agreed negotiated workplace agreement, then the workers' employment conditions as set by the negotiated agreement, must be better off than what is set in the Award.

Now the term *overall* scares me. It leads me to believe it is possible that some workers' employment conditions may not be 'better off' than the minimum standards set by an Award, particularly when the definition of what I think is a majority in a workplace. In my opinion, it may not be a majority due to the ballot numbers.

If we consider the ballot system for a new agreement, as discussed in Chapter Two, negotiated Agreements can be voted up with just over 1/3 of a workplace voting yes.

And say 25% of that workforce has their employment conditions altered unfavourably, then it's possible for some workers to have changes enforced by the overall workplace vote and possible to pass a BOOTs test as overall the remaining 75% conditions are better off.

Do not ask me how BOOT tests are applied – I have no idea. There are a lot better qualified people than me that can do that. Just know there is a test that is designed to protect workers, particularly vulnerable workers. But where there is a loophole, profiteers can exploit, in my opinion.

Workers deserve better, in my opinion.

Chapter Four

Hourly rate, composite rate, or an annual salary

Hourly rate

An employer may elect to pay us an hourly rate. An example could be for every hour we work, we will receive, hypothetically, $20.00 per hour.

If we work outside the spread of hours, as described in Chapter One, we may attract a penalty of, say, 25%.

To work this out, we calculate 25% of $20.00 and add the two together, which would be $25.00.

On most occasions, penalties are described as 125% for the example above.

Hourly rates are, in my experience, being used less and less but still need to be used for casual employment contracts.

Composite rate.

An employer may have negotiated to pay an hourly rate that can be termed as a composite rate. It has other names, but is usually called *composite* rate.

This means instead of earning $20.00 an hour for any hours worked, plus any penalties, we may earn, for example, $27.50 for every hour worked and no penalties.

The idea is that on average or over a working week or pay cycle, we will work some hours that could attract penalties and some hours that don't attract penalties. The higher rate is to compensate for the non-payment of penalties.

This system obviously has great advantages for an employer as it saves lots of time when calculating wages, as they don't have to work out hourly rates that may attract different penalty rates. It's one calculation of total hours worked multiplied by the hourly rate.

It can be a disadvantage for employees if some employees are rostered on hours that would never attract penalties, but they still get paid the higher rate, compared to an employee who is always working hours that normally would attract penalties but now under the composite rate don't receive them.

An example is that, when you work Monday morning, you get paid the same hourly rate as if you work a Sunday morning.

Under this system, the roster patterns have to be equalled and unsociable hours shared.

Annualised salary.

Using our chef's pay as an example: some employers pay an annualised salary. I will attempt to explain how it works for our chef, but it may vary from industry to industry. Read your Award or agreement.

An employer takes the hourly Monday to Friday

rate as set by an agreement or an Award then multiply that by 38 hours for the working week. Then multiply that amount by 52 weeks for the annual wage. So if our chef is earning $20.00 per hour.

$20.00 x 38 = $760.00 weekly, Monday to Friday rate
$760 x 52 = $39,520 Annual wage.

But chefs will work lots of weekends, late shifts, or early shifts, night shifts and public holidays, not just Monday to Friday.

So to work out the annualised salary, the employer calculates 25% of the annual wages of $39,520, which is $9,880. The employer then adds the annual salary and 25% of that annual salary together, which is $49,400.

The employer then takes this total figure of $49,400 and divides it by 52.

So the gross wages for our chef each week and every week of working over a year, based on the example above, is $950.

Our chef will take home this weekly wage if they work 50 hours or 38 hours or work all weekend, all public holidays or if they just work Monday to Friday.

Again, this system is great for employers as it saves time when working out wages each cycle.

In my experience, most employers don't, and most employees under this annualised system don't realise that every year, or at the point of employment termination, as I understand it, employers should balance out the hours worked to the minimum standards set by an Award.

This means that if an employee, our chef, would have earned more money under the minimum conditions set by an Award than they received under the annualised hours system. The employer should pay the difference.

In my opinion, it's only fair for this balancing process to occur.

As always, this is a rough guide to the wages system, and this is my experience. Other Awards or agreements may have different systems of variations to what I have described. The trick is to read your Award or Agreement.

Any questions call me.

Chapter Five

Workplace Health and Safety

I have been told that, statistically, in Australia, one worker dies every day from a workplace injury or illness. At first, I thought there had been a mistake – this figure seems way too high. However, when I started to think about illness from the workplace, like asbestos or long-term injury sustained in the workplace, then maybe it is possible: one worker a day may die from a workplace injury or illness.

While researching this, I found a federal government website showing figures that indicate on average, over a set period, one worker dies every three days from a workplace injury or illness.

We tend to only hear about the workers who die in workplace incidents, like crushing or falling injuries, and only in industries like agriculture, construction, and mining. I do not think it is newsworthy to say that Mr or Mrs John Citizen finally succumbed and died from his or her injuries or illness they sustained in a workplace ten years ago.

I also understand that a large proportion of deaths on our roads in crashes are from workers working. I cannot remember when or where that information comes from, so I cannot be 100% correct on its accuracy, but to a layman, which I am, it seems reasonable. Some of our road tragedies would have to be workers working.

Either way, if it's one worker a day, or one every three days, it's way too high.

So what is occupational or workplace health and safety?

In my opinion, it is about the employer and the employee working in a collaborative manner to ensure that all workers do not sustain an injury or illness in the workplace.

In my home state of Western Australia, there are two Acts that manage workplace safety. The *Occupational Health and Safety Act 1984* and the *Safety Regulations Act of 1986*.

The Act of 1984 created the WorkSafe Department and the general rules by which workplaces are required to operate, as well as other formal types of structures. It also established the basic responsibilities of the employer and the employee.

The 1986 Regulations Act, however, is a little more prescriptive to worksite safety. In a nutshell, this Act talks about first aid boxes in the workplace, as well as toilets and drinking water. It can be quite complex, particularly sections relating to chemicals. But both Acts need to be considered together.

A good employer will welcome the idea of keeping the employees safe. They do this by setting up safety committees, training safety reps, and listening to, and acting upon, concerns and ideas to keep workers as safe as possible.

In my experience, I know employers who will do anything to avoid all of this, such as appealing to a Safety Commissioner and the Minister of the Day, to avoid having a safety committee and talking with their employees. This happened to me in 2018.

I believe in each state, to ensure that Safety Acts are followed and to conduct investigations into safety, government departments have been created with inspectors. I have, in my time, contacted my local inspectors for support on matters relating to safety.

Workplace Health and Safety Legislation

It's not always clear, cut and dry who or which government department has jurisdiction for safety on a particular site. For example, when foreign ships pull into an Australian port and tie up to a Western Australian dock, is the ship in the jurisdiction of the Western Australian government, or the Federal government? Or is it the Australian Maritime Safety Authority (AMSA)? Or is it the ship's flag of origin? Say Panama? It can get murky.

Like all forms of legislation, it can be complicated and muddy at times, but I truly believe the intention of the legislation, if embraced, is good.

There are a couple of points in the Western Australian legislation that I always try to remember and share.

1. The IITS factor. Employers have a legislative reasonability to "Inform, instruct, train and supervise" all employees to ensure they are 'safe'. That's a pretty powerful statement, I believe.
2. All Personal Protective Equipment (PPE) is to be supplied free of charge. The number of employers I have experienced who do not do this is staggering, and the number of employers who only supply PPE after a probationary period has expired is also staggering.
3. The Hierarchy of Control. This is a system of how to manage a risk in the workplace. The following is the Hierarchy of Control which is a method the legislation suggests should be applied, in order of preference, from top to bottom.

    a) <u>Eliminate</u> the risk

    b) <u>Substitute</u> a system or plant for a safer system or plant. (*Plant* is a term used to describe all forms of equipment we use in a workplace. This ranges from a pen to a chair to a 50-tonne forklift)

    c) <u>Engineer</u> a safer system of doing a job e.g. install machinery guards.

    d) <u>Administrative</u> Change the way people work.

    e) <u>PPE Personal Protective Equipment.</u>

Risk and Hazards

There is always a question I find in safety when I hear both employers and workers talk about risk and hazards. What is the difference?

I have heard lots of explanations, but the one that works for me is this:

Risk is the energy

Hazard is what we are doing with that energy.

So, if I was climbing a ladder, the energy is gravity. The hazard is falling from height. We can't manage the energy in this example but we can manage the hazard of falling. We could lower the job, elevate the floor, use scissor lifts, or use elevated work platform harnesses and so on.

I have found, over the years, this explanation is not foolproof. It has some holes, but it's the best for me. Someone told me once that, for them, what worked best when trying to explain the difference between a risk and a hazard was, the risk was a shark, and the hazard was how deep I went into the water. Ankle deep ... not so bad, neck deep ... very bad. I'm still unpacking that one.

What's a Safety Rep?

A safety representative is an employee who has been nominated and elected as a safety representative in their workplace. This representative has a significant role in their workplace.

They can, and should, be involved in all safety investigations, attend safety meetings at regular intervals and represent fellow workers in safety issues and meetings.

Safety reps are normally voted into that position, but if there is only one person who has been nominated, then this person is elected unopposed. There are strict protocols in the time frames and ballot processes detailed in the legislation.

Safety reps must be trained, and this training is supplied by the employer. This is paid training and is usually completed over five days.

An elected position usually lasts just over two years. This position, in my opinion, is particularly important and requires extra work outside normal working hours. It can be confrontational at times and not just with the employer – also with workmates. A safety rep may have to side with the boss on a matter or enforce an unpopular system.

I urge all persons considering this role to think about all aspects of the job. It's hard work.

I am the nominated safety rep in my current workplace.

About ten years ago, I was a safety rep on the site of a large multinational transport company. This company used 50-tonne forklifts to move shipping containers around the site and on and off trucks. One day, a lifting chain from a 50-tonne forklift snapped and a 40 foot container weighing over 20 tonnes hit the ground. Only by luck, a truck and hence a driver was not under this falling load.

In this example, the risk (energy) was gravity, and the hazard was the suspended load falling.

As I was the safety rep, I investigated a lot of this

by myself as the incident was considered serious, but a fact of life, or normal occurrence in this industry.

I sat up one night and called the manufacturer of the forklift involved in the incident, who was located in America. I had them email me the maintenance schedules of this forklift, as well as the user manual.

On reading this information, I discovered that the stretch of the lifting chain was to be measured at certain intervals and that a special tool to complete this measuring was supplied with the forklift.

The WA legislation allowed me to inspect all maintenance reports on each forklift (which I did, much to the disgust of the maintenance department). I ended up being kicked out of the workshop for requesting these. I got them anyway and read them. Sure enough, the maintenance team was measuring the stretch, but I noticed that the chains never stretched after months and months of use.

On further investigation, it was discovered that the maintenance team was measuring the chain stretch in the wrong location. I believe it was behind the lifting cog, not in front of the lifting cog.

I walked into the workshop not long after this. I think 13 to 15 lift chains had been replaced on a fleet of 25 forklifts.

We're human, and we all make mistakes. We just must learn and move on. This investigation was hard, but it was worth it in the end.

Lastly, there are a lot of catchphrases in safety: 'zero target', 'everyone goes home safe', and 'who's waiting for you at home' etc. etc.

All these phrases have the right intention, but safety is not a catchphrase. It's a working, living, breathing thing being managed by humans, who at times get it wrong. We are all just trying to do the best we can with the experience and the knowledge we have.

Chapter Six

Workers Compensation

Workers compensation insurance is compulsory and is supplied by an employer to their workers in a workplace.

When a worker is injured or contracts an illness due to a workplace incident or event, and that worker can no longer work for a period as a result of this workplace injury or illness, they can still receive a supporting wage in the form of a benefit, called workers compensation. This payment is for a set period of time and amount.

It took me a long time to simplify the above down to one paragraph. The topic of workers compensation, in my opinion, is an extraordinarily complex system with detailed and highly complex forms of legislation. I understand that lawyers tend to specialise in this one field only. As said before, this is a chapter that could be a whole book and needs to be addressed by a specialist, not a simple layman like myself.

But I will share what I think I know about workers comp....

I believe that an injury – any injury – at work is very, very expensive, particularly for the worker and their family. In my experience, it can cost everything.

Now...if, after all the inductions, safety courses and meetings, you still find you become ill or injured at the workplace, and are unable to work as a result, then we have workers compensation insurance for all workers. I truly hope you never go here, and never for an extended period.

All workers should be covered by an employer's workers compensation insurance policy. This policy covers loss of wages and medical expenses, including rehabilitation and re-training to a new job if required.

Workers compensation insurance policy must be provided by law by employers to cover their workforce.

I understand the cost, or the premium of a workers compensation policy, is established by a few factors. The total amount of the gross wage is the major factor and then the risks associated with a particular industry. So office work and mining industries have very different risks associated with their duties, and therefore different premium amounts.

I have some experiences and personal philosophies on this topic that are especially important that most workers are not aware of or have not considered.

Workers Compensation Insurance policies are

provided by private enterprises who are usually more concerned, and frankly legally obligated, to make money or increase profits for themselves and/or their shareholders.

The care and well-being of an injured worker and their families, therefore, is not on the top of their priority list, in my opinion.

This, for me, is a little conflicting. I do not believe a health care system based on profit provides the best care for patients or workers. They simply clash.

There is a limited time frame and limited available funds for each successful workers compensation claim. I believe it is <u>two</u> years, and the prescribed amount for medical, wages and rehabilitation funds is approximately $300,000.

So a worker who falls from a height and breaks both their legs in that fall, and requires extensive treatment and rehabilitation, has approximately $300,000 available to cover all expenses and wages.

I met a man this had happened to. He worked in demolition and fell through a roof, resulting in multiple fractures to both his legs and hips. Funnily enough, we met doing our Certificate IV in Health and Safety at the time. He had to be retrained as he could no longer work in his chosen industry.

When we talk about time frames, we need to understand that there are several time frames in this process. These include how long we have to lodge a claim from the date the injury or illness occurred. The employer also has a timeframe to lodge the claim with their insurer, and the insurer has a time frame to accept or deny the claim.

After thirteen weeks of receiving wages which may include, for example, bonus overtime etc, the wage subsidy can be reduced to say, a Monday to Friday rate only. This (INSERT can) affects shift and weekend workers significantly.

There are many timeframes we need to be aware of, and the lag of time or delays between decisions can cost a family a significant amount – not just financially but also mentally and physically.

I understand that if after two years a worker is not back at work doing either normal duties or other duties, then the claim can be finalised.

Now, a reminder that the prescribed amount is approximately $300,000. This amount is to be used for the best interest of workers during the recovery process. I assume this amount is there to cover medical, retraining and rehabilitation expenses to help a worker get back to work as quickly as possible.

Workers need to remember that it is possible that every time a doctor calls a specialist to discuss a worker's compensation patients' treatment plan, they each can charge. These fees would be paid out of the total prescribed amount available for treatment and recovery.

Say, for example, you have three different doctors treating you. You could have a specialist or your GP doctor and the insurer's doctor having a chat to discuss your treatment. They will both be billing for this. Each doctor may charge a set amount per phone call, regardless of the length of that call.

These conversations, albeit important in a worker's recovery, can add up.

So workers who are in the system need to be aware of the limited funds available to you.

In 2020, I required stitches to my finger from a workplace incident. I was treated at a hospital Emergency Department and referred to a hand specialist to see if there was any nerve damage.

I travelled over 50 kilometres to this specialist, whom I never met. The nurse took a photo of my finger on her phone, sent it to the specialist, and I was told all was good. I was booked in for another appointment four days later.

The specialist then would have billed the insurance company what, I can only assume, would have been a significant amount of money for that snapshot.

In this experience of mine, I think some in the medical profession have missed the point. Workers compensation is for the worker protection and their safety net.

It appears at times to be considered as a 'cash cow' for treatment providers.

I never went back to that specialist appointment, and I registered a complaint with my employer on the treatment I was given. I hope they followed it up.

Workers should have the right to choose their own doctors and rehabilitation providers. If you need long-term care and treatment, then ask questions about costs and services provided so you can make an informed decision. I suggest that workers shop around or, if you need help, call me to discuss. I have met some great rehabilitation providers who will go into bat for workers and help protect the prescribed amount and ensure that the bulk of this amount is used for the worker.

It is important for you to know, however, that you cannot refuse to be medically examined by the insurance provider's doctor. There are limits on how many times and how often, but remember this:

> In the past, insurance providers have hired private investigators to covertly film and record workers they suspect are making false claims for workers compensation. If a worker is proven to have made a false claim, then I assume this is called *fraud* and is, most likely, illegal.

Indeed, the system has been exploited by some workers.

If there's an easy way to make easy money, workers, just like treatment providers, may not be immune to greed. But this behaviour only costs the genuine and those paying the insurance premium.

I would suggest that, in this multi-layer relationship between worker, employer, treatment provider and private insurance company, before you sign anything, you make sure you understand its consequences. The outcome could be significant and long term.

Prevention is better than cure. Participate in safety in your workplace and understand OHS and the safe systems at your workplace. Having a long-term injury can be drastic on you, your relationships and your well-being.

I believe the workers compensation system is designed to stop workers slipping through the gaps when an injury/illness occurs and this is a good thing.

It is not a perfect system – nothing is – but this is a supportive system and can be a good one if we involve ourselves in it, understand it and manage it.

Chapter Seven

Probation

Your new employer has the right to place you on a period of probation. This is common for employees appointed to permanent roles. Probation is a trial period between the employer and employee at the start of the employment contract; it is a test drive or a cooling-off period if you like.

The thing about probation is, either party can terminate the employment relationship without reason during the term of probation. At least one week's notice is required by either party unless an Award or agreement specifies a longer period (call me if you need help with this).

I find (and have found) that during probation, I walk around on eggshells, feeling insecure about my future and unsure about my performance. Good employers, in my opinion, will sit down regularly with new employees during probation and let them know how they are going.

This, for me, has certainly relieved the pressure of this insecure time. However, most employers never say anything and, when the probation period has expired, they just move straight over the date.

During a probation period, workers are extremely vulnerable to termination and changes to their conditions of employment.

There's a little catch that you should know about:

> under the <u>federal system</u>, employees *<u>do not</u>* have access to unfair dismissal laws until they have completed a minimum of six months of continuous service.

Quite often, I have seen letters of appointment, which include a probation period of three months. However, because new employees under the federal system cannot access unfair dismissal laws until six months of continuous services has passed, we are, realistically, all on probation for six months rather than three months.

State by State, or conditions under the state industrial systems may differ from the federal system. State systems, from what I have learnt, tend to closely follow the federal system. But it is worth double-checking as these laws can change regularly.

I believe that, during a worker's probationary period, an employer should not have the right to change or alter an agreement or contract negotiated during the recruitment period.

Here's an example to explain why. I once negotiated a rostering pattern with an employer prior to signing a contract in 2018. The negotiated roster allowed me to maintain my hours of work while at the same time meeting my family responsibilities.

I signed the contract based upon this understanding being agreed to.

Less than six weeks into my new position, the employer wanted to alter the agreement on roster patterns, which affected my family care responsibilities. My employer wanted more hours worked without increasing my pay.

Is this fair or reasonable? The employee has already negotiated with the employer the terms and conditions of their employment contract. Both parties have agreed to this and, whilst still on 6-month probation, the employment contract was changed.

What could I say? I needed the work. I agreed, and my family time suffered.

Probation is walking on egg shells for a 6-month period.

Chapter Eight

Letters of Offer

These types of letters are generally given at the start of any new employment contract and can come with many different names: 'Letter of Offer', 'Contract of Employment', 'Letter of Appointment' or 'Letter of Engagement'.

Whatever the name, a new employee should be given some sort of letter regarding their employment and conditions.

The information in these letters (or documents) is important and, by the employer supplying this information, disagreements in the future can be prevented.

A previous employer supplied me with a letter which you can read. It's a standard, normal and good letter of offer. It contradicts itself, in my opinion, but nonetheless, it's a clear contract.

I sometimes think employers think it works in their favour not to supply these types of letters, but I disagree. In my experience, not supplying these letters has caused nothing but trouble.

Also, these letters display professionalism and respect towards the new employee.

What these letters communicate, in a non-verbal way, is that my new employer is professional and demonstrates courtesy towards me.

As mentioned, these letters are (in my opinion) important and, as you can see from my contract, they should state the following:

* position you are being employed for
* start date (don't ever underestimate your start date and protect it; this may determine access to long service leave and redundancy payouts
* industrial instrument or Award that is being used to govern (or set) your terms and conditions of employment
* classification level you will commence at and the correlating pay rate
* your immediate supervisor or line manager and the department you will be employed in (this can be important so you can check if your classification is correct)

Additionally, you should be given at this time, or at least introduced to, policies in effect in your workplace.

If you don't get any form of a letter or you have concerns about what is written, call me. I am happy to help.

Chapter Nine

Employment Contracts

Permanent vs Casual

I think most workers and new ones understand the difference between full-time, part-time and casual employment. In a nutshell, a permanent employee, which is either in full-time or part-time employment, receives and accumulates entitlements such as sick leave and annual leave and has greater security in employment.

A casual employee does not accumulate these entitlements. In lieu of these entitlements, a casual employee receives a loading of 25% above their rate of pay.

So, for example, if your hourly rate of pay is $20 and you work 10 hours a week, your gross weekly income would be $250. $20 x 10 hours = $200 plus 25% loading is $50.

This casual loading of 25% is made up, as I understand it, of 20% to compensate for the entitlements given only to permanent employees (e.g. sick/annual leave), and 5% is originally a financial penalty or discouragement for employing casual employees.

So really, the main difference between casual and permanent is the engagement time. A casual is engaged for employment on an hour-by-hour contract. Theoretically, therefore, a casual can be terminated with only one hour's notice.

Set Contracts of Service

There is what is termed 'set contracts of service' or 'fixed term contracts', which are becoming more common, I believe. These contracts allow workers to be employed as a permanent employee with all the entitlements and of permanency, but only for a set period of time.

An example of when these contracts could be used is during periods of extended absences of a regular staff member, such as during parental leave, long service leave or a long-term injury or illness. They are also used in situations where the employment role only exists due to a funding grant or tender applied for and received by the employer/organisation. One last example is where a person is required to complete a particular job task that has an expected date of completion. Therefore, they set a fixed term for its completion.

These set types of contracts are, I believe, no longer being used for the purposes they were originally intended. It appears now these contracts tend to be used as a management tool for employers to avoid long-term relationships with their employees as these contracts are continuously rolled over.

Employment, and secure employment, is very

important to our economy, social standards and well-being. Security in employment should not be overlooked for a short-term financial gain, or because managers find it easier to 'flick staff' who are casual simply because they can't manage. There are specific laws that try to protect workers from this but, as is the case in industrial relations, it is complex stuff.

Recently there has been a push for conversion clauses in Awards for employees to seek secure employment. It is regarding conversion from casual employment to permanent employment. This push, in my opinion, has come about because employers were hiring and keeping employees on casual contracts for years, which is not to the benefit of the community overall.

So, if you are employed under a set term contract or on a casual basis and do not understand your rights, then please feel free to contact me.

If you are offered permanent full-time employment, I suggest you accept that and enjoy the benefits of secure long-term employment.

Chapter Ten

Workplace policies

Workplace policies are documents written by the employer, either with or without the involvement of the workforce. These policies can vary in topics – there can be one policy, or there can be hundreds.

These policies can touch on subjects that are either general in nature or specific to a certain worksite.

An example of a policy could be the uniform policy, or the drug and alcohol policy, social media policy, media policy, intellectual property policy, use of mobile phones in the workplace etc. etc. The list can go on and on

A copy of these policies should be made available to all employees or at least the employees should be informed where the policies are located.

Usually, when we start a new job, we can be asked to sign a document stating we have received the company's policies and that we understand them. Sometimes this is found in the letter of offer.

The reason for this is, as I understand it, that worksite policies can form a part of the employment relationship. If a worker fails to follow a policy or breaches a policy, it is possible their employment could be in jeopardy.

To break it down a little bit: a drug and alcohol policy I have experienced explained how the employer would test for any substances, the frequency of the testing, and what happens if an employee fails a test.

These documents can be altered and are usually reviewed on a set timetable. The employer should inform employees if a policy changes.

Policies are important tools of communication for an employer, and workers need to be aware of their existence and locations. Too often I have seen employees being terminated due to them not knowing a policy, or having signed a document saying they understood a policy but hadn't actually read it.

Take your time. Read them. Understand them, and ask questions if you are unsure.

There can also be a group of policies that overlap with other forms of legislation. For example, a safety policy or an inclusion policy. These documents are not restricted to just industrial documents.

Chapter Eleven

Leave

There are numerous types of paid leave available to most permanent contracted employees (not casuals) in our workplaces.

Like all things in industrial law, there is no one-size-fits-all. The type of leave and the amount of leave can and does vary from industry to industry and workplace to workplace.

Chapter Seventeen discusses what is called 'the NES National Employment Standards. Inside these eleven minimum employment standards available to all workers in Australia, it has eight sections or parts relating to a variety of leave entitlements.

These are annual, sick, carers, long service, bereavement, community, parental and domestic violence leave.

Most types of leave are accrued or earnt over a set period of time. For example, most workers receive a minimum of four weeks annual leave after a year of service. For a full-time worker completing a 38-hour week, this equals approximately 2.923 hours per week of service completed.

2.923 x 52 weeks = 151.996 hours. Divide 151.996 by 4 weeks, and we have 37.999 hours.

As I mentioned, the amount of leave available to workers can and does vary from workplace to workplace. Some variations occur as an incentive by employers to attract workers to isolation or remote workplaces. I recently worked on a 1.5 million acre cattle station in remote Queensland and six weeks annual leave was offered as an incentive.

Additionally, workers deemed to be 'continuous' shift workers can be entitled to an extra week's leave per year.

Again, we need to read and understand our Agreements, Awards, NES or even letters of contracts and company policies to establish our entitlements and access to leave.

In the past, annual leave attracted a 17.5% loading on top of the annual leave payment.

17.5% loading, as I understand it, came about because shift workers who would, over a week, complete shifts that would attract a variety of penalties or extra money for working outside of normal working hours, such as nightshift, weekends and public holidays. These shift workers discovered that when they went on leave, they suffered a loss in wages as their leave payment was calculated on the Monday to Friday rate only. So, shift workers successfully obtained a 17.5% leave loading to avoid this loss – an equalisation process. 17.5% loading eventually was awarded to all workers over the years.

Most workplaces I have worked in now no longer

have a 17.5% leave loading. It is claimed this payment is now in the annualised wages total.

Permanent workers can be entitled to ten days a year of sick leave, depending on if they are full-time or part-time employees. Which is usually also accrued over a term of service. The typical equation is ten days per twelve months service.

Most workers have access to Carers leave of two to three days, which can be paid or unpaid.

Carers and personal leave can, at times, be combined.

Carers leave is leave taken to care for an immediate family or household member. Who is an immediate or household member? There is a definition of 'immediate' family or household members in the NES' and most Awards also have a definition.

The term 'immediate' or household member, on occasion, is being challenged with attempts to expand who is covered by this clause. For example, pets are currently not included in this definition, but some argue they should be.

Personally, the current definition of who is immediate family or a household member is not very culturally aware, in my opinion.

Long service leave is accrued over a set period of years of service and is usually three months of paid time off. It is a reward to workers for their dedication of service to a particular employer.

I understand the history of long service leave is: it would take three months to travel to and back from

England/Europe in days gone by. I also understand we are one of only a few countries where long service leave is made available.

In the past, long service leave was made available after fifteen years of service but usually these days it's ten years of service. I have however read agreements where long service leave was available after only five years of service. Some employers might do this to attract and retain staff.

Long service leave in some situations can be transferable or portable from employer to employer.

This happens because some industries are very transient and workers have to work for multiple employers over time to remain employed.

An example may be the construction industry. Companies win and lose contracts and workers transfer from employer to employer to remain employed but, therefore, can miss out on long service leave on a regular basis. So long service leave could be portable or transferable.

Long service leave upon termination can be paid out as a pro-rata. For example, if a worker's employment is terminated at eight years and long service was available at ten years, the amount of long service leave available is payable at the time of termination.

This is done, as I understand it, to stop employers terminating employment prior to long service being accessed and paid for at, for example, the nine year and ten-month time frame.

Most leave accrues continuously or until taken or

used. For example, annual leave and sick leave continue to accrue year in, year out, until utilised. Most employers, however, do not like employees with large amounts of annual leave accruing and can and do request employees take leave at regular intervals.

Some leave does not accrue. I have worked in places where carers leave does not accrue. Domestic violence leave, as I understand it, does not accrue.

Some leave is payable at the time of termination. Annual and long service leave is payable, if applicable, whereas sick, carers and domestic violence leave is not usually payable at the time of termination.

Some workplaces have included that either a percentage of or the full amount of non-payable leave is payable at employment termination, in specific circumstances, such as redundancy or retirement.

Touching on domestic violence leave, which I wholeheartedly agree with but have one concern about. Usually, when we take leave, our payslips display the amount taken and the amount remaining. So, if an employer outlines domestic violence leave was accessed on a payslip, I believe this could cause an issue for a victim in most circumstances. They need to think about this.

Planned leave is subject to a specific term, which has caught me, and others, out at times.

Leave must be taken at a mutually agreed/convenient time for the employer and the employee. An employer needs to be able to staff up at busy times and can't have all staff away on leave at the same time.

In addition to reading and understanding leave entitlements from an Award or Agreement, we may need to possibly understand what a company's policy regarding leave may also have to say.

For example, a company policy may state that leave can only be accessed after twelve months of continuous service, or leave can only be taken in blocks of "x" number of days. Or, as previously mentioned, an employee can only accrue six weeks of total leave at one time.

So, my advice is, before you book tickets, accommodation, or make other plans regarding any planned leave, get your leave dates approved first.

This, of course, is for planned leave but not for unplanned leave, being sick and carers leave for example.

In my experience, Leave can and does change from workplace to workplace. All workers should read their agreements or Award and policies to establish their entitlements.

Any questions, feel free to contact me.

Chapter Twelve

Casual Conversion.

When I first started work, I was of the understanding that, after twelve months of being employed as a casual employee, I could ask for or I would be placed on a full-time contract.

I don't recall when, but workers lost this ability to transfer from casual employment to full-time employment, and workers could and, as far as I am aware, can remain a casual employee for decades.

Lots of workers, I believe, don't really appreciate the need for security in employment that a permanent position offers. Some, I believe, prefer casual employment as it means more money in their hand each week.

For me, this is an incorrect conclusion. The casual penalty rate is a calculation of entitlements that permanent employees receive at the time of accessing these entitlements and is not paid weekly.

So the cash amount is the same in the end, but the security is not, as a casual can be terminated without notice or reason with an hour's notice in most circumstances.

Now the NES (Chapter Seventeen) has a casual

conversion clause available to all Australian workers.

This clause, in very simple terms, means a casual employee can seek a conversion of their employment contract from a casual to a permanent employment contract after twelve months.

Now again, like all things industrial, it can be very complex.

For example, a casual employee attempting to seek conversion must be able to prove a continuous pattern of shifts and hours. The employer can argue that a conversion is not viable or could harm their business operations. The list goes on and on.

Regardless of the complexity, I would impress that the conversion is important, and all workers should be permanent.

At a minimum, understand that it's possible and that when your circumstances change, the conversion clause may help you.

Keep rosters, payslips and other information that may support a claim of conversion.

If you need some help, again, please feel free to contact me and let's have a chat.

Chapter Thirteen

Meetings

I have learnt and wish to share a few tactics over the years about having meetings with people and managers.

Managers should ask or contact you prior to a meeting being conducted, or at the least, it is a good practice to do so. In this correspondence, the manager should inform you why the meeting is occurring, what the topic of the meeting will be, and who will be attending.

The correspondence should outline the right of the worker to bring along any support person they wish to the meeting. However, in my experience, managers just call workers into a room without warning or reason for a quick chat, then the chat becomes a serious meeting. This is hard as the worker is not prepared or supported.

I have been called to these types of 'surprise' meetings in the past, now I do the following:

I ask, why are we meeting? Who is attending?

I have used the following script or words to this effect in the past.

> *"I am happy to meet with you and management at a mutually convenient time to discuss any matter. I would ask that I am offered an agenda or reason(s) for the meeting in writing at least 48 hours in advance. I would also request that I am offered a support person to be present if I so choose."*

Please note: I believe that no worker can just refuse to attend a meeting, regardless of how it is called. Attending a meeting at the request of an employer is possibly a lawful instruction. To just say 'no' could be failing to comply with a lawful instruction.

During the meeting, I suggest the following.

- **Tip one:** stay on topic. Many times, I have seen meetings drift off into something that was never put on an agenda or was the stated topic. If you find that a meeting is drifting, stop. Re-centre the meeting on the topic and start again.

- **Tip two:** suspend the meeting if you do not like what is happening and you feel threatened or intimidated. You have the right to suspend a meeting and seek help or a support person as you see fit. But do so in a calm and positive manner. You will need to reschedule the meeting and finish the process off at some stage.

For example: "I would like to terminate this current meeting and reschedule for another time as I feel I need support, *or* I am feeling threatened *and/or* intimidated."

- **Tip three:** Think about the time of day you want a meeting. Will it be better in the afternoon when they are tired and wanting to go home, or early in the morning when they are relaxed and happy? It will change with each event, with each person, and with each topic, but think about it.
- **Tip four:** ask for an agenda for the meeting, what is to be discussed, who is attending and their roles. This is a normal protocol and stops the 'surprise' meeting tactic. Then stay on topic.
- **Tip five:** be polite. Never swear, yell or just be a prick. It helps nothing
- **Tip six:** plan and take notes and get minutes drawn up and circulated. If no minutes are circulated, then send your own understandings of what the meeting was about and the conclusions reached.

Meetings can be hard but are also an effective tool of settlement and are a requirement. I always recommend a support person, either as a representative or as a witness, and never participate in a one-on-one if a sensitive topic is to be discussed at the meeting

My suggestions above about terminating meetings or requesting agendas etc., is nerve-racking to do. If you do follow my suggestions, remain calm.

Understand the difference between a support or representative person and a witness attending a meeting with you. A witness should not participate in the meeting. They are just that, a witness. A representative or a support person can and should participate in the meeting. Be clear on your desires for the support person attending.

Tips for committees

Have diversity on any committee. Young workers have different goals in negotiations to older workers who might be closer to retirement. Men and women can have different goals. Even workers with different ethnicity can have different goals. Embrace diversity.

One size does not fit all on committees.

Seek, listen and reply to the workers you are representing on a committee. Make sure the committee allows for some method for this to occur, either on noticeboards, by email or face to face, always report back on meetings. It makes for faster results from a committee if there is an effective report-back system in place.

When it comes to committees, the workers need to be sure that you are all on the same page. Have meetings before the committee meeting with management. Display unity, not diversion.

Chapter Fourteen

Employment Termination

There are four main ways that employment termination can occur, as I understand it:

Employee resignation

This is where an employee volunteers or elects to resign from their position for whatever reasons. They must give notice of resignation either verbally or in writing. It is usually stated in a contract or a workplace policy which method is preferred. The required length of notice for a resignation is stated in each particular industry-based Award or Workplace Agreement.

The resignation is usually decided by length of service, for example:

one year = one week's notice

2 to 5 years' service = two weeks' notice.

above 5 years of service = 4 weeks' notice.

If a worker fails to supply the required notice, an employer can have the right to withhold any money owing to the employee in lieu of notice.

An example would be if you resign from a position

and walk out the door immediately. If you had worked in that position for 5 years (and thus be required to give 4 weeks' notice) the employer could withhold any holidays or leave entitlements, including current week pay obligations, in lieu of that failed notice.

Employer termination

An employer may conclude that an employment relationship must end due to, for example, continual breaches of workplace policies, failure to complete a lawful task or instruction or a serious breach of workplace safety legislation.

Then the employer is possibly under the same obligation as an employee's resignation. They must supply notice as well (usually under the same requirements as the employee). If they fail to give notice, then the employer must pay for the time not given.

An example is where an employer terminates an employment contract and wants that employee gone, or off the worksite ASAP – this is usually the case as a disgruntled employee can be damaging to a working environment – the employer must pay all legal entitlements including leave, hours worked since last pay period as well as failed notice.

There is a belief that (INSERT all) employers must give 3 warnings prior to termination. I have never seen this as a legal requirement and it's not mentioned in any Award or agreement I have read, but it is certainly good managerial practise to do this.

I have, however, read the '3 strikes' system and grounds for immediate dismissal in workplace policies.

This means that different disciplinary and termination processes can be varied in different workplace.

Workplaces with a three strikes or warnings system in place should make sure that these only apply to the same issue or area of concern. It shouldn't be three different strikes make up the three warnings for termination. For example, three warnings on bullying is okay; but one on bullying, one for being continuously late and one for failing duties is not three warnings in a row in my opinion.

This is why I think the code of conduct policy in workplaces has become such a big policy covering a range of topics. This way warnings can be given on code of conduct rather than a specific event.

When issuing a formal warning, an employer should include information to help the employee understand why a warning has been given. They should also explain how they can improve their performance to avoid another warning. The employer should also offer to provide extra training or other tools to assist the employee to improve their performance.

It is poor management, I believe, to issue a warning letter and not explain what happened or how to improve the situation and avoid additional warnings and possibly termination.

If you are in a position of receiving a formal

warning, get help or representation. Be sure the lifespan of the warning is discussed and agreed. Usually, warnings can be for 12 months only. Warnings should not just sit over an employee's head indefinitely.

I have participated in a disciplinary meeting with an employee at a local council and he was given a warning for something – I cannot remember what – but I do remember it could have fallen either way with a warning letter or instant dismissal. It was a serious issue. The employee received a warning letter, and the employer wanted the letter to last for five years which, in my opinion, is overly harsh and unfair.

Redundancy

From time-to-time employers either downsize, restructure a workforce, or cease operations altogether. This can happen for many reasons: innovation, a reduction in market share and hence profit, or just broke and closing.

Whatever the reason, any employer can decide they need to make a position redundant from their workforce.

If an employer makes this decision, they can ask their workforce for volunteers to accept a redundancy package. This allows workers who were either thinking of retiring or moving on naturally, to apply for a redundancy package and move on. This method allows for less disruption and stress in a workplace and on employees and their families.

However, an employer can just make the decision

about which positions are to be made redundant and therefore force the redundancy. This can occur and is harsh and disruptive to all.

In the federal legislation there is a table of minimum applicable entitlements and notice to be given regarding redundancy.

For example, if you have completed 5 years' service, you may need to be given 4 weeks' notice of redundancy and possibly a redundancy payout of 8 weeks' pay.

You will find that redundancy payouts in these tables are capped at 10 years plus of service where a worker can receive up to 12 weeks' pay. This redundancy payment can increase with age, over 45s get a little more.

The table in the Act is the minimum entitlements and can be seen as a guide. When (and if) a workforce is negotiating an agreement, they could consider increasing redundancy payouts and time frames. I have seen agreed redundancy tables that extend to 25 years' service.

I think it's important to increase or attempt to increase these entitlements. Redundancy, particularly for older workers, can be devastating.

An employer should not replace a redundant position in a workforce for at least 12 months. This means that one day an employer should not make a position redundant and then the following day employ a worker to complete the same task and duties.

Basically, redundancy should not be used to

shuffle staff out the door and then re-employ a replacement the next day.

I have been in workplaces where employers have tried to avoid redundancy at all costs. They have offered re-deployment to another position within the company, provided additional training or job-sharing arrangements and so on, in a genuine attempt to avoid redundancy. I have also experienced workplaces where employers don't try to do any of this.

Usually, over the notice period, workers should be offered paid leave to attend job interviews and the like while seeking replacement employment. But this will often depend on what the Award or workplace agreement states.

Serious misconduct

As the name suggests, this is serious. If an employer starts to use this type of language, seek help. Serious misconduct is theft, fraud, fighting or drugs, to name a few, in the workplace.

If you have your employment terminated due to serious misconduct, as I understand it, you will forfeit any long service entitlements owing, notice of termination and payment in lieu of notice of termination payments.

Serious misconduct is difficult to defend, and, in my experience, is usually an illegal activity.

A good rule of thumb is: Don't break the law in

the workplace.

On the Sly

I have experienced, and very recently so, the way some employers just terminate workers 'on the sly' without dealing with any issues or dealing with a termination in a fair and just way.

As an example, I have experienced employers who just change set roster patterns so a worker cannot make a shift, or so it conflicts with other responsibilities. I call this 'managed out'.

An employer has the right to alter workplace patterns if they claim or prove the business needs to change to remain profitable, and so they should. But just to change agreements and/or rostering patterns and claim a need to do so for business needs and hence push a worker out the door is sly behaviour.

Another managed termination I have witness is, if you are a casual employee, a manager or owner can cut your hours significantly, making it impossible for you to meet your financial responsibilities. Your name can still appear on a roster, but you are not allocated any shifts. I call this 'starving a worker out'.

Something else I have learnt over the years: any worker, in my opinion, can be sacked or terminated at any time, with or without notice, regardless of any law in place.

I have seen for myself that it does not matter the length of service, the extra effort you have put in, the free work you have given, the accumulated sick leave you don't take, or basically the loyalty you have shown, when an employer has to choose between profit and loyalty, money usually wins.

Chapter Fifteen

Superannuation

Superannuation or 'super' is important, and a basic understanding of it is valuable.

Before I start this chapter, I need to say I am not a financial advisor or an expert in Superannuation, I am just sharing my personal experiences and thoughts. This chapter therefore cannot be considered financial advice.

I have been surprised how younger people in some workplaces I have worked in know very little about Super. I suppose retirement is not something we think about in our twenties. I guess we only really care about retirement and financial security when we see it on the horizon.

Super is a payment made by employers into an account that is made available to workers once they retire. Now, this is a basic definition of Super. However, like all things employment law-related, it is complex. For a detailed explanation and guidance with Super, I would ask an accountant, but here is my understanding of it, based on my experiences.

Currently the Super payment is 9.25% of gross

wages earnt in a 38-hour working week. This means that overtime and other wages and bonuses paid over and above the 38-hour week, may not attract Super payments. In some cases, however, these payments do attract Super.

Workers need to earn more than $450.00 per month to qualify for Super payments and be over a set age.

All workers, regardless of their employment contract – being casual, part-time or full-time – if they meet the criteria, they should receive Super payments.

Super should be paid into a worker-nominated Super account every quarter. I have received a letter from some employers when this payment has been paid, which I thought was a great thing, but this is rare.

As I said before, Super is designed to be a lump sum payment when workers retire so they can enjoy their retirement years and not rely on welfare.

In rare circumstances, early release of portions of your Super can be made, but this is only if people meet a set criterion of personal or financial hardship.

Most Super accounts also have some form of income protection, death and total or permanent disability insurance cover. It depends on your Super fund whether you are covered for these insurances.

I have seen the process where Super funds require you to opt out of an insurance policy, so in this situation you are automatically covered. This can be a good thing or a bad thing depending on your personal circumstances and the cost of the insurance policy that is drawn from your Super amount. Be informed and decide.

I recommend that each year workers phone up their Super fund(s), or register an online account, to confirm what insurances they are covered for and the price they are paying for this. When we are young and have little responsibilities, insurance could be seen as an expensive and unnecessary. Perhaps as we grow and our responsibilities change, these insurances become a more attractive option. But this is a personal choice, and it is not advice.

Workers can also nominate who receives their Super if they suffer an untimely death. Mine goes to my kids.

Each year, if you do a Super check, re-confirm your choices.

It is also worthwhile reviewing the performance of the fund. Workers should have the right to decide where their Super funds are invested. Personally, I don't like my Super involved or invested in what I see as unethical options. So, I am involved in choosing where my Super is invested, and I try to be sure it's invested in an ethical manner.

With approximately three trillion dollars of employee's Super funds invested in the Australian economy, workers could have a big say in the shape of the economy.

I would also recommend that you invite your Super rep to your workplace to give you all a presentation.

Super is very important, and our views change on

it as we move in age and experiences; but the earlier you start thinking about Super, the better off you will be in retirement.

Remember, Super is complex, and you should seek professional help and support when deciding what you should do with your Super.

Chapter Sixteen

Pay Rises and CPI

I think it's very important to discuss in basic terms at least, what Consumer Price Index (CPI) is and how this economic indicator affects pay rises for workers.

CPI is an indicator of the costs of goods and services that we, the consumers, purchase.

How do they work this out?

In layman terms it's simple, but of course in real life it's a lot more complex ... but I'm a layman.

Economists compare the cost of goods and services every three months by calculating the increase or decrease of these same goods. An analogy I have used over the years is that people all over Australia basically walk around the same supermarket buying the same goods every three months. They see if these products have increased, and if so, by how much.

Now, generally what is indicated in these shopping trips is that goods and services increase. Usually, a modest increase of anywhere between .1 of a percent to 1.5 of a percent.

In real terms this means that what a family could buy with $100 three months ago is more than what a family can buy with that same $100 today. The value (or purchasing power) of a hundred dollars goes down because goods and services go up.

In my opinion, we need to be compensated with pay rises at least every twelve months by an amount equal at least with the CPI indicator. If we don't achieve this, then, in effect, we are going backwards or taking a pay cut as the purchasing power of pay packets decreases as CPI increases.

Pay increases are important not just for us and our quality of life, but it also helps our economy, as any money or increases we achieve we tend to spend in shops anyway, stimulating growth and profits in our communities.

So, it's a circle and a very important circle.

This may seem a simplistic explanation, but I am just a layman after all and this book is about my experiences and knowledge.

Chapter Seventeen

The NES
(National Employment Standards)

Back in 2010, the federal government of the day embarked on an Award modernisation process. At the time, as I recall it, there was a reduction of Awards by a few hundred, and key terms and conditions were updated.

A part of this modernisation process was the creation of ten sets of employment conditions which were removed from Awards and placed into what's now called the National Employment Standards, or the NES.

These eleven minimum standards are available to every worker across every industry.

To name a few, these conditions include family friendly rosters or flexibility, overtime and the ability to refuse it, as well as parental leave, carer's leave and public holidays etc.

Really, it is the general employment conditions we all expect in our working lives that have been taken from individual awards and poured into one document.

I think the NES is a very important document and

as a minimum, every employee and worker should understand these basic entitlements. I also think the NES should be a living document and adjusted from time to time to reflect changes in our communities and workplaces.

It's available on the net, and I believe a copy needs and should be given to every new employee at the start of a new position. Don't just flick over it. Take the time to read it and understand this document and share this information with mates.

Chapter Eighteen

The 38 Hour Working Week and a Living Wage

The working week limit of a 40-hour week was reached decades ago and is based on three 8s.

8 hours work,
8 hours rest, and
8 hours play.

For me, this seems fair and reasonable.

Over time, however, the three 8's has been slowly eroding and most indicators point to workers doing a lot more unpaid or paid overtime and longer hours at work to get ahead.

Not too long ago, a weekly wage of 38 hours work was a living wage. In other words, the total amount received in wages was good enough to live on and meet weekly expenses. I would say that this is now no longer the case and most workers either must work overtime and other anti-social times in order to meet their household expenses.

Overtime and other entitlements were previously known as 'fruit' bonuses, used by workers to save for special treats like a holiday. I remember working these extra hours as a good way to save and get ahead.

These days, however, it appears that these entitlements are used just to stay afloat or to have a living wage.

We now see, I believe, a situation of wages stalling, living costs increasing, and workers falling further and further behind.

Most of us work a minimum of a 40-hour week, rather than a 38-hour week. I believe this came about because employer groups argued at the time it was too hard for them to manage a 38-hour working week. But, theoretically, we are only paid for 38 hours of work.

The extra two hours of work completed each week under the 40-hour system is often given as paid time off by adding the extra hours to annual leave or a paid RDO (rostered day off) to be taken at a mutually agreed time, or a half day every fortnight (usually a Friday).

But now even this seems to be eroding as well, particularly in the hospitality industry.

I would have thought that, as we move towards a more robotic or computerised workforce, leisure time would increase without loss of income, not decrease.

Overtime

Overtime, I believe, is any hours worked over a 38-working week.

In most Awards and agreements there are clauses that state 'an employee is expected to complete a reasonable amount of overtime'.

The question is here, what is reasonable?

I have worked for employers who think four hours a week is reasonable and others who think ten hours is reasonable.

I suppose the most important thing to know is that overtime can be refused, based on some personal commitments.

It is possible to say no to overtime due to OHS and family commitments. In my experience, employers just seem to think workers will do whatever hours they are told to do.

Personally, I believe that money is always available, particularly in Australia. But I cannot get time back. So for me, Time-off has always been more important than a few extra bucks. This is very much a personal decision and depends on your current circumstances.

Chapter Nineteen

Unions

What is a union?
In a nutshell, a union is a group of like-minded people working in the same industry or workplace, coming together to form an organisation, or a union, with the view of improving the group's common employment goals.

These goals could be money or wages, safety, time off or even community standards. The members of this union pay a membership fee to the organisation (or the union), so the union can operate, employ workers, have offices and pay the power bill etc.

Unions can, and do, represent their members at meetings with management regarding a variety of matters. They also represent their members at times in the industrial relations law courts. Workers' unions lobby governments to help improve the working lives of their members.

A long time ago, the workers unions in Australia got together and formed the Trade Union Council of Australia, which is the body that speaks for all unions. Basically, it is the union for unions. It makes more sense to have one lobby group hitting up politicians rather than 30 different unions knocking on the door with the same, or similar, message.

Unions have, and do, play, in my opinion, a very important role in our workplaces and have helped create our workplaces as we know them today. For example, they have played a significant role in establishing the 38-hour working week, superannation, days off, paid holidays and safety.

Here is an example of a union we may all know:

This union is extremely high profile, always in the media, defending its members and having its say; influencing its industry that runs into billions of dollars. I also think it has 100 percent membership: the AFL Players Association. This union represents members who play AFL football at the top level.

It's not a union by name but I believe it's a union by model. Its goals and its outcomes are exactly the same as any workplace union. Think about that for a minute. They are like-minded individuals that join and pay to belong to a membership-based group to advance their careers and entitlements.

Another example of some pretty powerful unions influencing governments and shaping our workplaces are employers' unions, or what employers like to term 'representative bodies': Australian Hotels Association or AHA, Australian Retail Association and Australian Mines and Minerals Association or AMMA to name a few. Again, the same model as a worker's union. Employers pay a fee to belong to a body of like-minded individuals to advance their common goals.

The big difference I see between the two types of

unions – workers and employers union – is the president or the chair of these employer associations are employed, whereas workers' unions chairs are elected. But I could be wrong.

Again, think about this: employers' unions are liked-minded, pay a fee for membership to advance their common goals.

I see no difference between employers' unions or associations and workers unions. The systems appear to be similar in membership or objectives. But, in my opinion, workers' unions are demonised by media and politicians.

Now workers unions have been, I believe, in decline for a long period of time. This decline in membership also seems to be at the same time as what I see is a decline in workers' entitlements.

It's your choice to be a union member or not. It's your choice to be an active union member or not, but consider this:

Can you as an individual or an individual employer stand-up, be heard and improve working life or profits alone against an employer or a government? Or is it better for a group of workers or a group of employers to stand up together to try and improve their working lives.

I am a union member and I have always been a union member. I like the voice it gives me in a range of topics in my workplace, as well as in my community. Unions have been at the forefront of change in a range of social issues.

But it's your choice.

Chapter Twenty

Bullying

In recent years, our society has seen a significant increase in awareness being raised about what bullying is and its impacts in general. This can be only a good thing.

Workplaces have very much been included in this cultural shift; however, they have their own unique characteristics and involve circumstances I think need to be addressed and understood separately. At the very least, there are factors which need to be considered prior to someone making an accusation of bullying within the workplace.

Like all things in workplaces, it's a little bit of a mine field.

What bullying isn't

Employers, managers, and supervisors have a legal right to instruct and discipline employees when and if a workplace breach of Award, agreement or policy has occurred.

Additionally, employers, managers and supervisors have the right to manage a business, to adjust and change business activities in response to market forces or leadership decisions and choices.

This management of business activities is broad, from calling meetings, changing operating times, to reducing or increasing the size of a workforce.

Awards and enterprise bargaining agreements have clauses regarding the introduction of change in the workplace and the steps that should be followed when introducing significant change.

A legal instruction to complete a task is not necessarily bullying. Its how an instruction is given that may constitute bullying.

My definition of bullying

This is a pretty broad definition but in the past, it has provided me with a good starting point to work with when analysing if alleged workplace bullying is occurring or not.

> *Workplace bullying is an ongoing pattern of behaviour that a worker finds to be threatening, intimidating and/or unwelcoming.*

One word in this statement which acts as a benchmark for me is *'pattern'*. Is there a pattern or repetitive behaviour that is or has occurred and how do you prove a pattern of behaviour?

If we make an allegation, we must supply the evidence to substantiate that claim.

My advice is to keep a workplace diary. I keep a journal of every job I have worked. These days it is an Excel spreadsheet with my start and finishing times, who I worked with and any events that occurred over the day that I think should be recorded. These events are also a trigger for me to remember the shift.

I would recommend that everyone keeps a work journal or dairy.

If you believe you are being bullied, you should always make sure you have a trusted ally with you in all meetings and interactions with the alleged perpetrator. And keep a record.

Bullying in any form, in any community interaction, is intolerable and unacceptable. Seek support and help if you are suffering, from whomever you feel safe with

I have memories of working and being bullied. Anyone can be a victim.

Chapter Twenty-one

Payslips

Whenever a worker receives their pay, the employer must provide a pay slip. The pay slip is a summary of earnt wages by the employee.

There are legal requirements regarding what information must go into payslips. These include employee's name, employer's name and ABN (Australian Business Number), pay period, date of payment, gross and net wages.

What is meant by gross and net wages?

Gross wages are the total amount of wages (or money) you have earned before taxes and other deductions.

Net wages is what we take home, or the amount of money we physically receive.

The payslip needs to also include another range of information, including: any loadings or penalties received, hourly rate, the number of hours worked in the pay period and Super contributions paid or set aside to be paid by the employer on your behalf.

Deductions

Payslips need to detail all deductions an employer

withholds on your behalf. There are a range of deductions, the first being income tax or PAYE or PAYG (Pay As Your Earn or Pay as you Go income tax) which is a federal government tax that all working Australians pay.

Other deductions could be employee self-contributions to their Super, social club or union fees etc. The most important bit of information to know is that all deductions need to be on the payslip.

What doesn't have to be included but is handy to know!

Payslips will generally display a record of leave entitlements (most commonly it will show annual and sick leave both accrued and taken to date).

Funnily enough, employers are not, as I understand it, legally required to include on payslips the amount of annual or long service leave accrued nor any entitlements remaining.

It seems a little strange that this leave is a legal entitlement, yet employers are not legally required to disclose the amounts regularly on an employee's payslip. The formulas of accrual are in most Awards and can be worked out if your payslips do not display your entitlements, but usually there are 4 weeks a year of annual leave and 10 sick days.

I once asked an employer why they didn't supply this information and they told me they feared if workers knew how much leave entitlements they had, they would access that leave.

I'm not sure how this theory works. Employees

can still access their leave if they elect to do so.

Annual, long service and other leave entitlements accrues or accumulates. At the end of the employment relationship, any annual leave entitlements should be paid out. After a set period of time – usually after 7 years of continuous service, but this can change from Award to Award and Agreements – long service leave should be paid out.

Accrued sick and carer's leave usually is not paid out at the end of an employment relationship but again, it can be depending on what has been negotiated in a collective agreement. I have seen at retirement or redundancy accrued sick leave or a portion of it is paid out, say 75%.

Personally, I am not a fan of paid out sick leave. I have experienced workers who don't take this leave when they are sick hoping to have a larger payout, and this is not what sick leave is designed for. If you are sick, stay home, get better and get paid.

Lots of employers do elect to inform their workers of leave entitlements and it is considered best practice to do so. If your payslips fails to tell you this information, then use this as a guide:

- 4 weeks paid leave each year for full-time workers, pro rata for part-time, and no leave entitlements for casual
- 10 days sick leave each year for full-time workers, pro rata for part-time workers and zero for casuals
- 2 days paid or unpaid carer's leave

for full-time and pro rata for part-time workers, zero for casuals

- 10 days paid or unpaid domestic violence leave for all workers

Pro rata means a proportion of that whole amount.

Consider the following scenarios:

I work 19 hours a week and my co-worker works 38 hours a week as a full-time employee. This means I work .5 of a full-time 1.0 load. Another example is if I work 4 days a week and my co-worker works 5 days a week as a full-time employee, then I work a .8 of the full-time 1.0 load (or hours).

Entitlements to leave are considered 'pro rata' to, or are a proportion of, what a full-time employee is given. Going back to the previous scenarios: leave amounts for the part-time employee would be 50% and 80% of what a full-time worker would get. So instead of 4 weeks paid leave, they would be entitled to either 2 weeks (50%) or 3.2 weeks (80%) paid leave.

These leave entitlements can change from workplace to workplace and roster systems. For example, some employers use extra leave entitlements to attract workers to isolation employment. Or a roster pattern that includes night shift or unsociable hours can attract an extra week's leave.

You will need to check your Award, Agreement of employment contract to confirm your entitlements.

Again, everything written here is a guide based on my personal experiences.

Chapter Twenty-two

The Gig Economy.

As I understand it, the gig economy is not a new system of employment but is becoming a much wider used system of employment.

In short, I believe the system of the gig economy is that a worker earns an income from a provider of good and services by sharing a certain percentage of the sale of those good or services to a customer.

The system side steps all the entitlements a worker would and has enjoyed for decades. Like paid sick leave, paid holidays, superannuation, access to unfair dismal laws, safety etc.

On paper, the worker is deemed to be a self-employed individual and the relationship between the provider and the worker is deemed not a traditional employer-employee relationship.

Taxi drivers decades ago would share a percentage of the daily takings with the provider of the taxi. So the concept of ride-share providers sharing a percentage of the takings is not, in my opinion, a new system.

It appears that the concept of sharing the takings is expanding to other industries.

Is it right or wrong? I am not sure. I have a personal choice to work in an environment where I am provided by laws to be safe, to earn entitlements and to have access to a free court system if need be.

But my choice may not work for everyone.

I understand that here in Australia, and around the world, the Gig economy is being challenged in the courts for a variety of reasons.

If you elect to work in a system of the gig economy, or a system where turnover is shared, you will need to read a detailed contract and understand the full implications of that contract. If this is your choice, then I can still help. Contact me to discuss.

Email: howworkworks@gmail.com

www.ingramcontent.com/pod-product-compliance
Lightning Source LLC
Chambersburg PA
CBHW030042100526
44590CB00011B/305